PUFFIN BOOKS

WHAT A WONDERFUL DAY!

Special days come throughout the year, with Christmas, birthdays, Easter, pancake day and Hallowe'en. And then there are those other special days that you can remember so clearly, a trip to the seaside or joining the fun at a carnival, throwing the coloured waters at Holi, and Aunt Louise's wedding. In this anthology Leonard Clark, Gareth Owen, Robert Louis Stevenson and Odette Thomas, along with many others, celebrate those wonderful days that can never be forgotten.

Tony Bradman is a well-known journalist, anthologist and author of children's books. His other books in Puffin include *Smile Please!*, *The Mad Family* and *Animals Like Us*. He was also the founder of the Best Books for Babies competition. He is married with three children and lives in Kent.

D1783664

Other books by Tony Bradman

WHAT A WONDERFUL DAY!

Poems chosen by
TONY BRADMAN

Illustrated by Madeleine Baker

PUFFIN BOOKS

PUFFIN BOOKS

Published by the Penguin Group
27 Wrights Lane, London W8 5TZ, England
Viking Penguin Inc., 40 West 23rd Street, New York, New York 10010, USA
Penguin Books Australia Ltd, Ringwood, Victoria, Australia
Penguin Books Canada Ltd, 2801 John Street, Markham, Ontario, Canada
L3R 1B4
Penguin Books (NZ) Ltd, 182-190 Wairau Road, Auckland 10, New Zealand

Penguin Books Ltd, Registered Offices: Harmondsworth, Middlesex, England

First published by Blackie and Son Ltd 1988
Published in Puffin Books 1990

1 3 5 7 9 10 8 6 4 2

This collection copyright © Tony Bradman, 1988
Illustrations copyright © Madeleine Baker, 1988
All rights reserved

Made and printed in Great Britain by
Richard Clay Ltd, Bungay, Suffolk NR35 1ED

What a Wonderful Day!

Days may come, and days may go,
Some bring rain; and some bring snow.
Some bring laughter, some bring tears;
They turn to weeks, then months, then
  years.
Some bring birthdays, presents and
  smiles,
On some we travel miles and miles
To holiday places in the sun,
Where there is sea, and sand, and fun.
Some days are spooky, like Halloween,
And some are the best you've ever seen.
Carnival, Christmas, a day at the zoo . . .
Special for someone, special for *you*.
These are the times when you just want
  to say:
Oh, what a wonderful, *wonderful* day!

Tony Bradman

The New Year

I am the little New Year, ho, ho!
Here I come tripping it over the snow,
Shaking my bells with a merry din—
So open your doors and let me in!

Presents I bring for each and all—
Big folks, little folks, short and tall;
Each one from me a treasure may win—
So open your doors and let me in!

Some shall have silver and some shall
    have gold,
Some shall have new clothes and some
    shall have old;
Some shall have brass and some shall
    have tin—
So open your doors and let me in!

Some shall have water and some shall
    have milk,
Some shall have satin and some shall
    have silk!
But each from me a present may win—
So open your doors and let me in!

Anon

A Piper

A piper in the streets today
Set up, and tuned, and started to play
And away, away, away on the tide
Of his music we started; on every side
Doors and windows were opened wide
And men left down their work and came
And women with petticoats coloured like
  flame
And little bare feet that were blue with
  cold
Went dancing back to the age of gold.
And all the world went gay, went gay,
For half an hour in the street today.

Seumas O'Sullivan

The Pancake

Mix a pancake,
Stir a pancake,
　　Pop it in the pan.
Fry the pancake,
Toss the pancake,
　　Catch it if you can.

Christina Rossetti

Pancakes

Pancakes!
Pancakes!
Don't let the pancakes
Frizzle away!

Pancakes!
Pancakes!
Pancake Day!
If you don't give us any
We'll all run away.

Anon

I Love the Friday Night Smell

I LOVE THE
friday night
smell of
mammie baking
bread———creeping
up to me in
bed, and tho
zzzz I'll fall

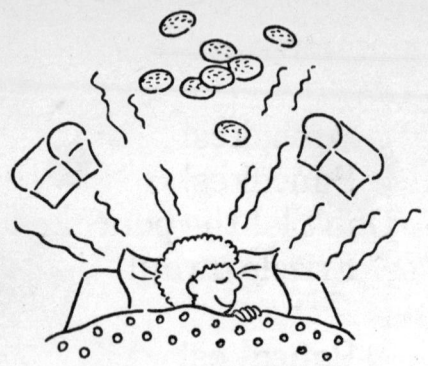

asleep, before I
even get a
bite——when
morning come,
you can bet
I'll meet a
kitchen table
laden with
bread, still
warm and fresh
salt bread
sweet bread
crisp and brown
& best of all
coconut buns
THAT'S why
I love the
friday night

smell of mammie
baking bread
putting me to
sleep, dreaming
of jumping from
the highest branch
of the jamoon tree
into the red water
creek
beating calton
run & catching
the biggest fish
in the world
plus, getting
the answers right
to every single
sum
that every day
in my dream
begins and ends
with the friday
night smell of
mammie baking
bread, and
coconut buns
of course.

Marc Matthews

On Mother's Day

On Mother's Day we got up first,
so full of plans we almost burst.

We started breakfast right away
as our surprise for Mother's Day.

We picked some flowers, then hurried
   back
to make the coffee—rather black.

We wrapped our gifts and wrote a card
and boiled the eggs—a little hard.

And then we sang a serenade,
which burned the toast, I am afraid.

But Mother said, amidst our cheers,
'Oh, what a big surprise, my dears.
I've not had such a treat in years.'
And she was smiling to her ears!

Aileen Fisher

An Egg for Easter

I want an egg for Easter,
A browny egg for Easter;
I want an egg for Easter,
So I'll tell my browny hen.
I'll take her corn and water,
And show her what I've brought her,
And she'll lay my egg for Easter,
Inside her little pen.

Irene F. Pawsey

Easter Eggs

Some strange bird lays chocolate eggs
Filled with smaller eggs or chocolate
   drops,
Not in grass or a tree or a hedge,
But on the shelves and in the windows
   of shops
And the nest isn't straw lined with
   feathers
But a coloured cardboard box.

Stanley Cook

Patience

Chocolate Easter bunny
   In a jelly bean nest,
I'm saving you for very last
   Because I love you best.
I'll only take a nibble
   From the tip of your ear
And one bite from the other side
   So that you won't look queer.
Yum, you're so delicious!
   I didn't mean to eat
Your chocolate tail till Tuesday.
   Oops! There go your feet!
I wonder how your back tastes
   With all that chocolate hair.
I never thought your tummy
   Was only filled with air!
Chocolate Easter bunny
   In a jelly bean nest,
I'm saving you for very last
   Because I love you best.

Bobbi Katz

Minnie and Mattie

Minnie and Mattie,
  And fat little May,
Out in the country,
  Spending a day.

Such a bright day,
  With the sun glowing,
And the trees half in leaf,
  And the grass growing.

Pinky white pigling
  Squeals through his snout,
Woolly white lambkin
  Frisks all about.

16

Cluck! Cluck! the nursing hen
   Summons her folk,
Ducklings all downy soft,
   Yellow as yolk.

Minnie and Mattie
   And May carry posies,
Half of sweet violets,
   Half of primroses.

Violets and primroses,
   Blossoms today
For Minnie and Mattie
   And fat little May.

Christina Rossetti

Full Moon

Full moon is the nicest time
For telling 'Nancy story
Except the ones 'bout snake and ghost
Because they are so scary

Hide and seek is nice then too
Because it's light as day
And mamas don't say it's too late
If you go out to play

Odette Thomas

Holi, Festival of Colour

Throw the waters, coloured waters,
Holi Festival's here.

Musicians playing, drummers beating,
Processions leading through the streets.

Joyfully children dance and sing,
Holi the colourful Festival of Spring.

Friends and relations all will meet,
Sweetmeats, balloons, for when they greet.

Throw the waters, coloured waters,
For Holi Festival's here!

Punitha Perinparaja

Aunt Louise's Wedding

Today I'm being a bridesmaid,
I'm wearing a dress that's blue;
I've got a big bunch of flowers,
And a pair of bright shiny shoes.

Everyone's looking excited,
It's such a wonderful day;
But why are *both* grannies crying?
And *what* did Uncle Jim say?

The vicar was very boring,
At least, that's what Dad said.
Mum said Dad should have whispered,
Then she belted him right round the
   head.

My auntie, the bride, looked so pretty,
It was nice when we had to sing.
But oh, what a commotion!
The best man said he'd lost the ring.

Later, we all had a party,
And my mum and dad had a row.
Both of my grannies were crying,
And one of my grandpas was, now.

Everyone was getting tired,
The food and the drink were soon gone;
My flowers were looking wilted,
The day had been very long.

I really loved being a bridesmaid,
It was such a wonderful day . . .
But I don't think I want to get married;
At least, not quite in that way!

Tony Bradman

Fathers Are Quite Important

When Dad got up this morning,
He acted rather strange.
He chuckled, and he smiled a lot
(At least that made a change).

At breakfast he kept looking
Under all the cups and plates,
And with a wink he said he knew
Why we should make him wait.

By lunchtime Dad was looking grim,
He said, 'A joke's a joke.'
He told us that he liked a laugh,
And said, 'I'm quite a decent bloke.'

What could he mean? We wondered,
What was he on about?
And why was our Dad cross now?
Why did he start to shout?

'Fathers are quite important,
Dads are nice,' he said.
We'd hardly time to say 'Quite right!'
Before he'd gone to bed.

We wondered, and we wondered—
Why had Dad been that way?
You don't think . . . it couldn't, could it . . .
Have been . . . Father's Day?

Tony Bradman

Carnival in Trinidad

Romance in the tropic air
Here and there and everywhere
Everyone is on the go,
Pans to tune, costumes to sew;
Money lending
Wire bending
Metal sheeting
In the beating
Bleachers building,
Coaches gilding.
Miles of gold and silver braid
Heralding the masquerade.

Ancient monarchs, ladies fair,
Dragons belching red hot air,
Grotesque mok-jumbies tall
Red Indians, wigwams and all
Groggy fellow
Strumming cello
Police chasing
Children racing
Parents hissing
Lovers kissing . . .
All part of the masquerade.

Nydia Bruce-Solomon

Tomorrow's the Fair

Tomorrow's the fair,
And I shall be there,
Stuffing my guts
With gingerbread nuts.

Anon

The Roundabout

Round and round the roundabout,
Down the 'slippery stair'—
I'm always to be found about
When circus men are there.
The music of the roundabout,
The voices in the air,
The horses as they pound about,
The boys who shout and stare—
There's such a lovely sound about
A circus or a fair.

Clive Sansom

26

I Meant to Do My Work Today

I meant to do my work today—
But a brown bird sang in the apple tree,
And a butterfly flitted across the field,
And all the leaves were calling me.

And the wind went sighing over the land,
Tossing the grasses to and fro,
And a rainbow held out its shining
    hand—
So what could I do but laugh and go?

Richard le Gallienne

The Parade

Drums beat,
Bugles blow,
Sirens sound,
Balloons
Burst with a bang,
Bells ring,
Pipes play,
People sing.

All the traffic stops
Or has to go a different way
And people line the road
On the day of the big parade.

Men march,
Girls dance,
All the vans,
Carts and lorries
Are in fancy dress.

I sit on my father's shoulders
So I can see.
I wave to the parade
And from the lorries
That look like castles,
Space ships,
Monsters,
Houses,
Or desert islands,
Everyone waves back at me.

Stanley Cook

At the Zoo

There are lions and roaring tigers, and
    enormous camels and things,
There are biffalo-buffalo-bisons, and a
    great bear with wings,
There's a sort of a tiny potamus, and a
    tiny nosserus too—
But *I* gave buns to the elephant when *I*
    went down to the Zoo!

There are badgers and bidgers and
  bodgers, and a Superintendent's
    House,
There are masses of goats and a Polar,
  and different kinds of mouse,
And I think there's a sort of a something
  which is called a wallabaloo—
But *I* gave buns to the elephant when *I*
  went down to the Zoo!

If you try to talk to the bison, he never
  quite understands;
You can't shake hands with a mingo—he
  doesn't like shaking hands.
And lions and roaring tigers hate saying,
  'How do you do?'—
But *I* give buns to the elephant when *I* go
  down to the Zoo!

  A. A. Milne

Haytime

It's Midsummer Day
And they're cutting the hay
Down in the meadow just over the way,
The children all run
For a frolic, and fun—
For haytime is playtime out in the sun.

It's Midsummer Day
And they're making the hay
Down in the meadow all golden and gay,
They're tossing it high
Beneath the June sky,
And the hay rakes are spreading it out to
 dry.

Irene F. Pawsey

In a Wonderland

A boat, beneath a sunny sky
Lingering onward dreamily
In an evening of July—

Children three that nestle near,
Eager eye and willing ear,
Pleased a simple tale to hear—

In a Wonderland they lie,
Dreaming as the days go by,
Dreaming as the summers die:

Ever drifting down the stream—
Lingering in the golden gleam—
Life, what is it but a dream?

Lewis Carroll

Seaside

Barefoot on the hard wet sand
Run and run,
The world is just awake, stretching
In the sun,
As far as we can see, the beach lies
New and clean,
Shining with stones and shells, jewels
For a Queen.

Look, a starfish rocking gently
In a pool.
Catch it—put it back again
Safe and cool.
Play until the tide comes up
Foaming white
To wash the sand smooth again
In the night.

Jennifer Andrews

The Paddling Pool

If you find a paddling pool,
Dabble your toes to make them cool.
   Splash! Splash! Splash!
Kick up your feet and scatter the spray,
Oh what fun for a bright sunny day!
   Splash! Splash! Splash!

E. M. Adams

At The Seaside

When I was down beside the sea
A wooden spade they gave to me
    To dig the sandy shore.
My holes were empty like a cup,
In every hole the sea came up
    Till it could come no more.

Robert Louis Stevenson

The Dancing Horse

In a place where we wanted to be
In the country near the sea,
The harvest festival had begun
And very busy was everyone.
Heaps of tulums and lollipops,
Sugar cakes and orange drops,
Lemonade and ginger ale,
Icy cold, were all on sale.
There were tries for several games
And many people with different names.
Then the steel band began to play
And everyone was alive and gay:

Even a horse in the Police Force
Who seemed to sing, 'Of course, of course,
To this music I will certainly dance.'
He snorted with a sprightly prance—
 Clop, clop, hoppity hop,
Three turns before a stop.
Riding the horse was Constable Lyle
Who sat upright but had to smile.
He loved his horse and did agree,
A dancing horse is a joy to see.
All the people who were there did say:
'The dancing horse was the best of the
 day.'

Daphne Pawan-Taylor

My Party

I'm giving a party tomorrow at three,
And these are the people I'm asking to
  tea.

I'm sure you will know them—they're old
  friends, not new;
Bo-Peep and Jack Horner and Little Boy
  Blue.

And Little Miss Muffet, and Jack and his
  Jill
(Please don't mention spiders—nor
  having a spill).

And Little Red Riding Hood—Goldilocks
  too
(When sitting beside them, don't talk of
  the zoo).

And sweet Cinderella, and also her
  Prince
(They're married—and happy they've
  lived ever since!)

And Polly, and Sukey; who happily settle
On each side of the hearth, to look after
  the kettle.

All these are the people I'm asking to tea;
So please come and meet them tomorrow
  at three.

Queenie Scott-Hopper

Happy Birthday, Dilroy!

My name is Dilroy.
I'm a little black boy
and I'm eight today.

My birthday cards say
it's great to be eight
and they sure right
coz I got a pair of skates
I want for a long long time.

My birthday cards say,
Happy Birthday, Dilroy!
But, Mummy, tell me why
they don't put a little boy
that looks a bit like me.
Why the boy on the card so white?

John Agard

It's My Birthday

It's my birthday today,
And I'm nine.
I'm having a party tonight,
And we'll play on the lawn
If it's fine.
There'll be John, Dick and Jim,
And Alan and Tim,
And Dennis and Brian and Hugh;
But the star of the show,
You'll be sorry to know,
Will be Sue.
(She's my sister, aged two,
And she'll yell till she's blue
In the face, and be sick.)

Anon

Betty at the Party

'When I was at the party,'
  Said Betty, aged just four,
'A little girl fell off her chair
  Right down upon the floor;
And all the other little girls
  Began to laugh, but me—
I didn't laugh a single bit,'
  Said Betty seriously.

'Why not?' her mother asked her,
  Full of delight to find
That Betty—bless her little heart!—
  Had been so sweetly kind.
'Why didn't you laugh, my darling?
  Or don't you like to tell?'
'I didn't laugh,' said Betty,
  'Cause it was me that fell.'

Anon

Croptime

It is croptime
And the chimneys
Are smoking, are smoking;

And the carts,
Heavy-laden,
Are groaning, are groaning.

Little children
The sweet canes
Stand sucking, stand sucking,

While the clear juice
Down their elbows
Is dripping, is dripping.

I shall sit here
And gaze at
Kites flying, kites flying.

Will you join me?
For it's cool with
Wind blowing, wind blowing.

Vilma Dubé

'Punkie-Night'

Here come children
On Punkie-night
With mangold-lanterns,
And candle-light
Gleaming inside
The goblin-faces'
Yellowy grins
And gold grimaces.
In and out
Of Hinton St George,
By church and hostel,
By farm and forge,
Swinging their gargoyle
Mangolds bright,
There go children
On Punkie-night.

Eleanor Farjeon

This Is Halloween

Goblins on the doorstep,
   Phantoms in the air,
Owls on witches' gateposts
   Giving stare for stare,
Cats on flying broomsticks,
   Bats against the moon,
Stirrings round of fate-cakes
   With a solemn spoon,
Whirling apple parings,
   Figures draped in sheets
Dodging, disappearing,
   Up and down the streets,
Jack-o'-lanterns grinning,
   Shadows on a screen,
Shrieks and starts and laughter—
   This is Halloween!

Dorothy Brown Thompson

45

A Halloween Pumpkin

They chose me from my brother: 'That's t
Nicest one,' they said,
And they carved me out a face and put a
Candle in my head;

And they set me on the doorstep. Oh the
Night was dark and wild;
But when they lit the candle, then I
Smiled!

Dorothy Aldis

Bonfire Night

All day like a bonfire
The sun is alight
But glows and goes out
In the cold dark night.

The wind makes fireworks
Of the autumn trees
That scatter showers
Of red and yellow leaves.

And I have a bonfire
That like a fiery dragon
Eats the guy
And roars in the garden.

And I have rockets
That shoot up high
With extra stars
To add to those in the sky.

I use my sparklers
To write my name
And the fireworks paint the night
With coloured flames.

Stanley Cook

November the Fifth

And you, big rocket,
  I watch how madly you fly
  Into the smoky sky
  With flaming tail;
  Hear your thin wail.

Catherine wheel
  I see how fiercely you spin
  Round and round on your pin;
  How I admire
  Your circle of fire.

Roman candle,
　I watch how prettily you spark
　Stars in the autumn dark
　Falling like rain
　To shoot up again.

And you, old guy,
　I see how sadly you blaze on
　Till every scrap is gone;
　Burnt into ashes
　Your skeleton crashes.

And so,
　The happy ending of the fun,
　Fireworks over, bonfire done;
　Must wait a year now to remember
　Another fifth of November.

Leonard Clark

It's Christmas

Carols drift across the night
Holly gleams by candlelight
Roaring fire; a spooky tale
Ice and snow and wind and hail
Santa seen in High Street store
Television . . . more and *more*
Mince pies, turkey, glass of wine
Acting your own pantomime
Socks hung up. It's Christmas time!

Wes Magee

The Christmas Party

We're going to have a party
    And a lovely Christmas tea,
And flags and lighted candles
    Upon the Christmas tree!

And silver balls and lanterns,
    Tied on with golden string,
Will hide among the branches
    By little bells that ring.

And then there will be crackers
    And caps and hats and toys,
A Christmas cake and presents
    For all the girls and boys.

With dancing, games and laughter,
    With music, songs and fun,
We'll make our Christmas party
    A joy for everyone!

Adeline White

Questions on Christmas Eve

But *how* can his reindeer fly without
  wings?
Jets on their hooves? That's plain
  cheating!
And *how* can he climb down the chimney
  pot
      When we've got central heating?

You say it's all magic and I shouldn't ask
About Santa on Christmas Eve.
But I'm confused by the stories I've
  heard;
      I don't know what to believe.

I said that I'd sit up in bed all night long
To see if he really would call.
But I fell fast asleep, woke up after dawn
      As something banged in the hall.

I saw my sock crammed with apples and
  sweets;
There were parcels piles high near the
  door.
Jingle bells tinkled far off in the dark;
    One snowflake shone on the floor.

Wes Magee

Christmas Morning

On Christmas mornings
I wake up to see
What Father Christmas
Has brought for me.
Wrapped in my blanket
Like a cocoon
I wonder if this time
I've woken too soon.
Perhaps my stocking
Of blue and white
Will still be as empty
As it was last night.
Is it too early to take a peep?
But I'm too excited
To go back to sleep.
I crawl in the dark
To the foot of the bed
My heart bumping softly
With excitement and dread.
And yes! He's been,
There can be no doubt
The stocking's all bulges
When my hand reaches out.

When my family crowd shouting
In through my door
I know that Christmas
Has come round once more.

Gareth Owen

Christmas Stocking

What will go into the Christmas Stocking
While the clock on the mantelpiece goes
   tick-tocking?
     An orange, a penny,
     Some sweets, not too many,
     A trumpet, a dolly
     A sprig of red holly,
     A book and a top
     And a grocery shop,
     Some beads in a box,
     An ass and an ox,
     And a lamb, plain and good,
     All whittled in wood,
     A white sugar dove,
     A handful of love,
     Another of fun,
     And it's very near done—
     A big silver star
     On top—there you are!
Come morning you'll wake to the clock's
   tick-tocking,
And that's what you'll find in the
   Christmas Stocking.

Eleanor Farjeon

Christmas Mornings

Up in the morning, early
sunlight on the cold floor,
nobody singing on far hills,
animals quiet, something in the air,
a touch of frost on the window sills,
a father standing by the door,
a mother smiling there,
a baby sleeping in the morning early.

Up in the morning, early
firelight on the warm floor,
everybody singing on the near hills,
whole house alive, something in the air,
a lick of rain on the window sills,
father standing by the door,
mother laughing there,
me waking in the morning early.

Leonard Clark

Christmas Thank You's

Dear Auntie
Oh, what a nice jumper
I've always adored powder blue
and fancy you thinking of
orange and pink
for the stripes
how clever of you!

Dear Uncle
The soap is
terrific
So
useful
and such a kind thought and
how did you guess that
I'd just used the last of
the soap that last Christmas brought

Dear Gran
Many thanks for the hankies
Now I really can't wait for the flu
and the daisies embroidered
in red round the 'M'
for Michael
how
thoughtful of you!

Dear Cousin
What socks!
and the same sort you wear
so you must be
the last word in style
and I'm certain you're right that the
luminous green
will make me stand out a mile

Dear Sister
I quite understand your concern
it's a risk sending jam in the post
But I think I've pulled out
all the big bits
of glass
so it won't taste too sharp
spread on toast

Dear Grandad
Don't fret
I'm delighted
So *don't* think your gift will
offend
I'm not at all hurt
that you gave up this year
and just sent me
a fiver
to spend

Mick Gowar

Index of First Lines

Acknowledgements

The author and the Publishers would like to thank the
following for their kind permission to use copyright material
in this anthology:

The Bodley Head for 'Happy Birthday, Dilroy!' from *I Din
Do Nuttin* by John Agard, illustrated by Susanna Gretz;
The Estate of Leonard Clark for 'November the Fifth' and
'Christmas Mornings' by Leonard Clark; Stanley Cook for
'Bonfire Night' from *Come Along* by Stanley Cook and for
'Easter Eggs' and 'The Parade'; Charles Scribner's Sons for
'August Afternoon' by Marion Edey from *Open the Door*;
David Higham Assocs Ltd for 'Punkie-Night' and
'Christmas Stocking' from *The Children's Bells* by Eleanor
Farjeon; Aileen Fisher for 'On Mother's Day' from *Ship
Around the Year*; The Society of Authors as the literary
representative of the Estate of Richard le Gallienne for 'I
Meant to Do My Work Today' by Richard le Gallienne;
Collins Publishers for 'Christmas Thank You's' from *Swings
and Roundabouts* copyright © Mick Gowar; Bobbi Katz for
'Patience' copyright © 1979; Wes Magee for 'It's Christmas'
and 'Questions on Christmas Eve'; Marc Matthews for 'I
Love the Friday Night Smell'; Methuen Children's Books
and McClelland and Stewart Ltd, Toronto for 'At the Zoo'
from *When We Were Very Young* by A A Milne; Collins
Publishers for 'Christmas Morning' from *Song of the City*
copyright © Gareth Owen 1985; Punitha Perinparaja for
'Holi, Festival of Colour' from *Festivals 3* (Oxford University
Press); A & C Black for 'The Roundabout' by Clive Sansom
from *Speech Rhymes*; Bogle-L'Ouverture Publications Ltd
for 'Full Moon' by Odette Thomas from *Rain Falling, Sun
Shining*; Random House, Inc for 'This is Halloween' by
Dorothy Brown Thompson from *The Random House Book of
Poetry for Children*.